TRAVIS AND MOLLIE
AND
THE ENCHANTED FLUTE

Written and Illustrated by Libby Nickel with Barbara Gay
Copyright 2017 by Just Fun Books & Things.
4991 Manor Ridge Lane, San Diego CA 92130
All Rights Reserved. Printed in the United States of America.
No part of this publication may be reproduced or distributed in any form or by any means, or stored in a database or retrieval system, without the prior written permission of the publisher.
ISBN 978-0-9990471-1-8   LCCN 2017904802

Travis and Mollie like to take walks around the neighborhood with Grandpa and Grandma.

They know their neighbors and enjoy seeing most of them.

They get lots of attention, pats on the head, and nice comments about what good dogs they are!

The neighbors who live in the house near them go to work every day, so Travis and Mollie don't see them on their daytime walks.

However, they know they have a cat named Mew that never goes outside.

The neighbors next to Mew's house have one dog. He is named Mojo.

He is much bigger than Travis, and he is very friendly.

Sometimes, Travis and Mollie hear pleasing music coming out of this house. They don't know what it is, but they are learning more about it every day.

Travis and Mollie can understand many words, such as come, stay, wait, no, time to eat, bedtime, go potty, good dog.

They can also hear and understand the words coming from a musical instrument someone has at Mojo's house. The instrument is telling a story, and this is the story they hear and can understand.

My name is Bundy. I know this because the name, Bundy, is engraved on the main joint of the flute. I am a silver colored tube with all kinds of holes, covers, and levers that can be pressed to make music.

This is my story.

In a Midwestern town many years ago, the local school's music director was starting a music program for all of the schools in his district.

Becky was a young fifth grader then, and she heard the news.

She asked her mother if she could learn to play a horn.

Becky's mother talked with Mr. Parker, the music director.

He suggested that Becky learn the flute.

Although the flute was expensive, Becky's mom bought a new flute that happened to be named Bundy.

Becky always called me by my name—she never called me just flute.

Although Becky had played a recorder, a whistle-type instrument, in the fourth grade, she was surprised to find playing a flute was not so easy.

I, Bundy, had to be coaxed to make a sound.

There was much blowing until Becky became dizzy and frustrated before a sound finally came out! Then, finally, there was a note.

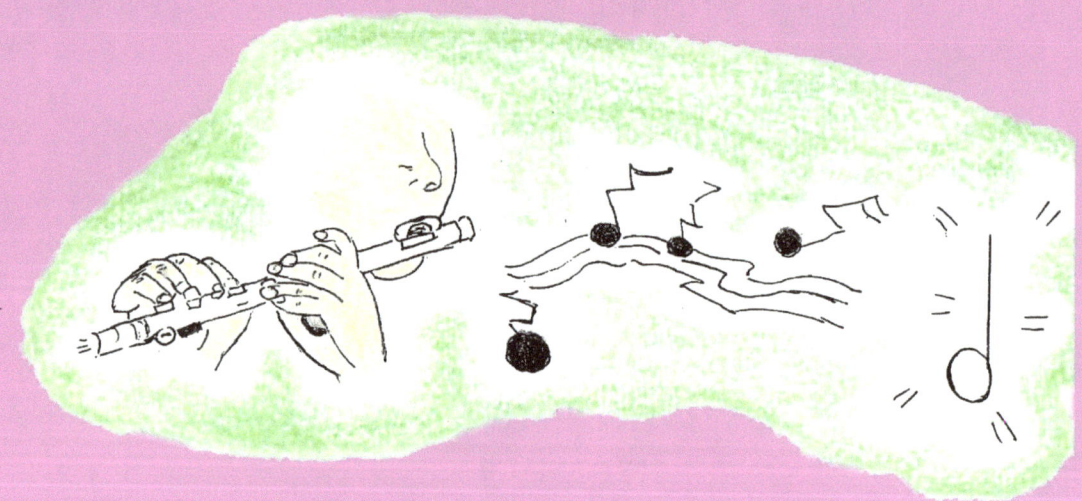

I knew then that Becky was on the right track.

Some mornings before school, Becky and I would go to the music room in the high school to practice with kids from all of the elementary schools.

This was a beginner's band, and it was quite noisy! But Becky and I were learning to play together.

After band practice, Becky would walk back to school with Marylou and Tommy.

Both Marylou and Tommy's clarinet cases had handles. My case did not.

Becky would hold me in my case close to her heart where I could keep warm.

It was a pleasant trip back to school where I rested in the coat room until time to go home.

As time went by, Becky stayed with the band.

We played in the concert band and in the marching band.

It was hard to read the notes while marching. Becky memorized the songs so she could see where she was going. I was thankful that we had no collisions with the drummers or other instruments!

I am a little guy compared to the sousaphone—a special marching band bass horn!

When high school was finished, Becky did not take me with her when she went away to college.

I stayed in her parents' home and slept in my case on the top shelf of her closet.

Later, when Becky became a bride and moved to a new home, she took me with her.

However, she did not take me out of my case for a long time, and I went back to sleep.

I was awakened several times as I was moved to closets in new houses.

One time, I even heard children laughing and playing! I just went back to sleep for a long, long time.

One day I heard Becky talking to me as she opened my case. She was no longer a girl! She wore glasses, and she looked like a mother or grandmother-type of lady.

She had gray hair, and she looked very lonely. Her children were grown and gone. Her husband was no longer alive.

I thought she looked very lonely and needed a friend like me.

Becky put me together and tried a few notes. I had many squeaks, squawks, and sour notes!

She said, "Looks like we will start at the beginner level again, Bundy."

So she conquered dizzy spells and all beginner's problems.

We practiced often and slowly, but we were making progress.

I was thrilled and found that I was beginning to sound like my old self again!

One day at the Senior Center Becky discovered another lady who had played flute in her high school band many years ago. Becky and Lucy, her friend, started meeting weekly to practice and have a little tea party to make the time an enjoyable venture.

I was glad that Becky seemed to be back in the music world, only on a different plane. We played Christmas carols at the Senior Center. It seemed to be a success, and Bundy Flute was very proud of his ladies.

Since Becky had kept me all of these years, she decided it was time to buy another flute for a backup in case I, Bundy, had to go to the shop for repairs. This seemed to be a good move, because there was a time that another flute was needed.

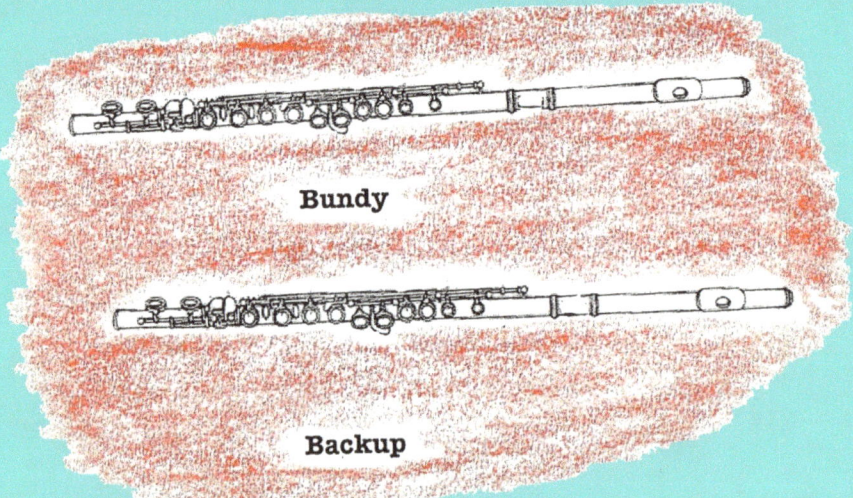

A young girl named Stephanie, who was about the same age as "Young Becky," came to visit. I learned that Stephanie stayed with her grandmother and grandfather during the week so she could go to school on a regular schedule.

Her grandmother helped Steph apply and get accepted to a special school that had many classes in music, arts, and drama. Becky offered to loan me to Stephanie so she could learn to play the flute. I was no longer a backup flute! I was Steph's only flute.

Steph seemed very excited about learning to play the flute, but she found me to be a challenge.

Becky knew that she had to be Stephanie's teacher-trainer. The first task was to show Steph how to assemble or put me together.

The flute comes in three parts—the head joint, the middle joint, and the foot joint. Stephanie had to learn how to carefully hold me without bending my levers—which are called keys.

During the first lesson, Stephanie had many trials before I could make a sound.

There was much huffing and puffing that led to tears and a major meltdown!

But finally she could make the first note! Oh Joy! Joy! Joy!

Day after day Steph kept at it until more pleasant notes were filling the room. She was so patient and determined. I was cheering for her as she continued playing my beautiful notes.

Steph kept stumbling over Becky's name. She would call her Grandma, and then say she was sorry. Finally, we decided that Becky would be Grandma Becky, and Lucy would be Miss Lucy.

This settled the problem.

Miss Lucy and Grandma Becky decided to have a Flute Recital. The two ladies asked Steph and me to join them. We are now The Fabulous Flutes!

I still go to school with Steph and love to go to Grandma Becky's house to practice and play on special occasions with our Fabulous Flutes!

'Ole Bundy' can still make a young girl happy. Two young girls and just one flute--Me, Bundy--have made a difference in Becky and Stephanie's lives.

Travis and Mollie enjoy seeing Mew and Mojo on their walks, and they hope Bundy, the Enchanted Flute, will delight others by sharing his story of Becky, Lucy, Stephanie, and the Fabulous Flutes!

JUST FUN
Books & Things

For Marcus, Chiara, Sonja, Leilani, and their children.

Thanks to the following:
    Ray, David, and Astrid for their patience and help to the writer while working on this book.
    Jeanette for her help in designing related products.
    All of the Humane Societies and other pet shelters who rescue, care for, and find good homes for all animals who need their help.

This book was inspired by the activities of Travis and Mollie--dogs who are owned, cared for, loved, and spoiled by the writer and her family. Travis was bred by Tropico Kennels in Palmdale, CA. Mollie was adopted from the Rancho Coastal Humane Society in San Diego, CA.

For information on other related books or products, contact JUST FUN Books & Things at justfun1936@gmail.com or by phone at (858) -342-3816.

www.ingramcontent.com/pod-product-compliance
Lightning Source LLC
LaVergne TN
LVHW072102070426
835508LV00002B/236